The Drowsy Hours

POEMS *for* BEDTIME

The Drowsy Hours

POEMS *for* BEDTIME

Selected by Susan Pearson ✤ *Illustrated by Peter Malone*

HarperCollins*Publishers*

The Drowsy Hours: *Poems for Bedtime*

Compilation copyright © 2002 by Susan Pearson

Illustrations copyright © 2002 by Peter Malone

Page 40 represents an extension of the copyright page.

Printed in Hong Kong. All rights reserved.

www.harperchildrens.com

Library of Congress Cataloging-in-Publication Data

The drowsy hours: poems for bedtime / selected by Susan Pearson ; illustrated by Peter Malone.

p.   cm.

ISBN 0-688-16603-2 — ISBN 0-06-029421-3 (lib. bdg.)

1. Night—Juvenile poetry.   2. Children's poetry, American.   3. Children's poetry, English.

4. Bedtime—Juvenile poetry.   5. Sleep—Juvenile poetry.   6. Lullabies, American.   7. Lullabies, English.

[1. Night—Poetry.   2. Bedtime—Poetry.   3. Sleep—Poetry.   4. American Poetry—Collections.

5. English poetry—Collections.   6. Lullabies.]   I. Pearson, Susan.   II. Malone, Peter, 1953– ill.

PS595.N54 D76   2001   2001024355   811.008'033—dc21   CIP   AC

Typography by Robbin Gourley and Jeanne Hogle

1 2 3 4 5 6 7 8 9 10

❖

First Edition

CONTENTS

Nightfall

One by one
that dark magician
Night
folds the colors of the day
like scarves
and hides them
in his sleeves

We run
holding our balloons
of no color
We run through the park
and the dark grass
grows shadows of
deeper dark   In the flower beds
every flower
is gray   The fountain
is a drifting ghost

Night
that dark magician
is racing us home
stopping only to turn off
the merry-go-round
with its little black horses
blockprinted
on the empty scene

BARBARA JUSTER ESBENSEN

The Starlighter

When the bat's on the wing and the bird's in the tree,
Comes the starlighter, whom none may see.

First in the West where the low hills are,
He touches his wand to the Evening Star.

Then swiftly he runs on his rounds on high,
Till he's lit every lamp in the dark blue sky.

ARTHUR GUITERMAN

The Mouse

I heard a mouse
Bitterly complaining
In a crack of moonlight
Aslant on the floor—

"Little I ask,
And that little is not granted.
There are few crumbs
In this world any more.

"The bread-box is tin
And I cannot get in.

"The jam's in a jar
My teeth cannot mar.

"The cheese sits by itself
On the pantry shelf—

"All night I run
Searching and seeking,
All night I run
About on the floor.

"Moonlight is there
And a bare place for dancing,
But no little feast
Is spread any more."

ELIZABETH COATSWORTH

Open Range

Prairie goes to the mountain,
    Mountain goes to the sky.
The sky sweeps across to the distant hills
And here, in the middle,
    Am I.

Hills crowd down to the river,
    River runs by the tree.
Tree throws its shadow on sunburnt grass
And here, in the shadow,
    Is me.

Shadows creep up the mountain,
    Mountain goes black on the sky,
The sky bursts out with a million stars
And here, by the campfire,
    Am I.

KATHRYN AND BYRON JACKSON

Baby Toes

There is a blue star, Janet,
Fifteen years' ride from us,
If we ride a hundred miles an hour.

There is a white star, Janet,
Forty years' ride from us,
If we ride a hundred miles an hour.

Shall we ride
To the blue star
Or the white star?

CARL SANDBURG

Wynken, Blynken, and Nod

Wynken, Blynken, and Nod one night
  Sailed off in a wooden shoe,—
Sailed on a river of crystal light
  Into a sea of dew.
"Where are you going, and what do you wish?"
  The old moon asked the three.
"We have come to fish for the herring fish
  That live in this beautiful sea;
  Nets of silver and gold have we!"
     Said Wynken,
     Blynken,
     And Nod.

The old moon laughed and sang a song,
  As they rocked in the wooden shoe;
And the wind that sped them all night long
  Ruffled the waves of dew.
The little stars were the herring fish
  That lived in that beautiful sea—
"Now cast your nets wherever you wish,—
  Never afeard are we!"
  So cried the stars to the fishermen three,
     Wynken,
     Blynken,
     And Nod.

All night long their nets they threw
　　To the stars in the twinkling foam,—
Then down from the skies came the wooden shoe,
　　Bringing the fishermen home:
'Twas all so pretty a sail, it seemed
　　As if it could not be;
And some folk thought 'twas a dream they'd dreamed
　　Of sailing that beautiful sea;
　　But I shall name you the fishermen three:
　　　　Wynken,
　　　　Blynken,
　　　　And Nod.

Wynken and Blynken are two little eyes,
　　And Nod is a little head,
And the wooden shoe that sailed the skies
　　Is a wee one's trundle-bed;
So shut your eyes while Mother sings
　　Of wonderful sights that be,
And you shall see the beautiful things
　　As you rock in the misty sea
　　Where the old shoe rocked the fishermen three:—
　　　　Wynken,
　　　　Blynken,
　　　　And Nod.

EUGENE FIELD

The Moon's the North Wind's Cooky

(What the Little Girl Said)

The Moon's the North Wind's cooky,
He bites it day by day,
Until there's but a rim of scraps
That crumble all away.

The South Wind is a baker.
He kneads clouds in his den,
And bakes a crisp new moon *that . . . greedy*
North . . . Wind . . . eats . . . again!

VACHEL LINDSAY

Someone

Someone came knocking
    At my wee, small door;
Someone came knocking,
    I'm sure—sure—sure;
I listened, I opened,
    I looked to left and right,
But nought there was a-stirring
    In the still, dark night;
Only the busy beetle
    Tap-tapping in the wall,
Only from the forest
    The screech owl's call,
Only the cricket whistling
    While the dewdrops fall,
So I know not who came knocking
    At all, at all, at all.

WALTER DE LA MARE

Questions at Night

Why
Is the sky?

What starts the thunder overhead?
Who makes the crashing noise?
Are the angels falling out of bed?
Are they breaking all their toys?

Why does the sun go down so soon?
Why do the night-clouds crawl
Hungrily up to the new-laid moon
And swallow it, shell and all?

If there's a Bear among the stars
As all the people say,
Won't he jump over those Pasture-bars
And drink up the Milky Way?

Does every star that happens to fall
Turn into a fire-fly?
Can't it ever get back to Heaven at all?
And why
Is the sky?

LOUIS UNTERMEYER

The Frog

How nice to be
       a
       speckled
       frog
with all those
       colors
       in
       a
       bog
AND SIT THERE ALL DAY LONG AND SOG
how nice at noon
to keep so cool
just squatting in your private pool
or when enough of THAT you've had
       to sun
       on
       your own lily pad.

But best of all at rise of moon
with you
and all your friends
in tune
as *jug-o'-rum*
and *jing-a-ring*
and thrilling *peep-peep-peep*
you sing
till
    listening
        we
          fall
            asleep
              slowly
           listening
          fall
asleep.

CONRAD AIKEN

The Bridge

A bridge
by day
is steel and strong.
It carries
giant trucks that roll along
above the waters
of the bay.
A bridge is steel and might—
till night.

A bridge
at night
is spun of light
that someone tossed
across the bay
and someone caught
and pinned down tight—
till day.

LILIAN MOORE

The Gentle Giant

Every night
At twelve o'clock,
The gentle giant
Takes a walk;
With a cry cried high
And a call called low,
The gentle giant
Walks below.

And as he walks,
He cries, he calls:

"Bad men, boogie men,
Bully men, shoo!
No one in the neighborhood
Is scared of you.
The children are asleep,
And the parents are too:
Bad men, boogie men,
Bully men, shoo!"

DENNIS LEE

The yellow fog…

The yellow fog that rubs its back upon the window-panes,
The yellow smoke that rubs its muzzle on the window-panes
Licked its tongue into the corners of the evening,
Lingered upon the pools that stand in drains,
Let fall upon its back the soot that falls from chimneys,
Slipped by the terrace, made a sudden leap,
And seeing that it was a soft October night,
Curled once about the house, and fell asleep.

T. S. ELIOT from "The Love Song of J. Alfred Prufrock"

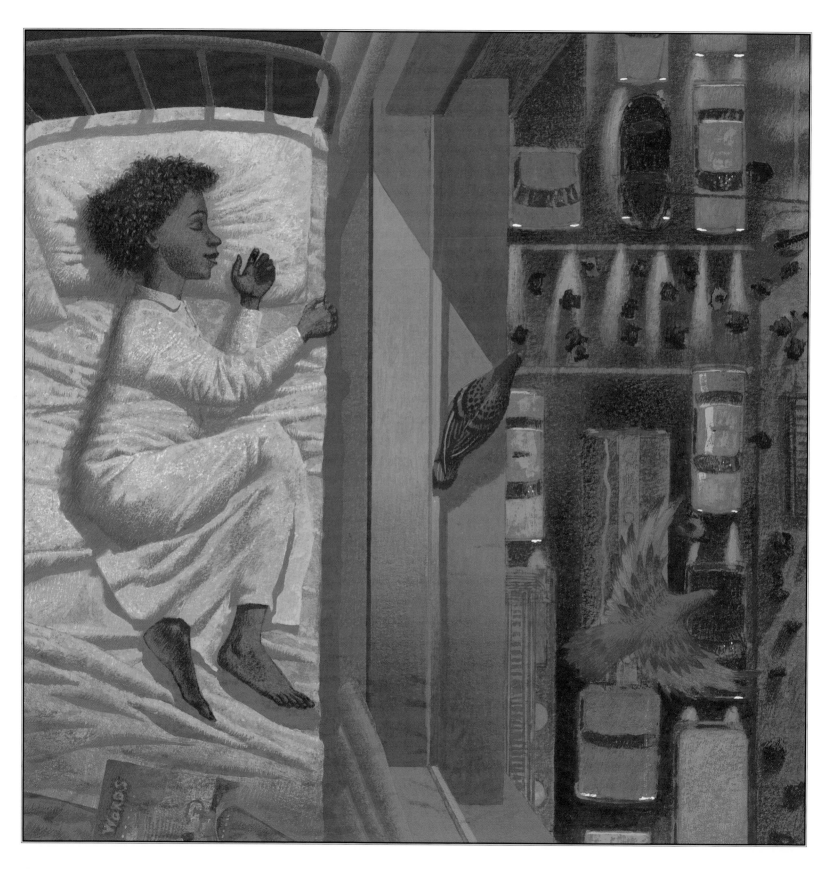

Manhattan Lullaby

Lulled by rumble, babble, beep,
let these little children sleep;
let these city girls and boys
dream a music in the noise,
hear a tune their city plucks
up from buses, up from trucks
up from engines wailing *fire!*
up ten stories high, and higher,
up from hammers, rivets, drills,
up tall buildings, over sills,
up where city children sleep,
lulled by rumble, babble, beep.

NORMA FARBER

Windy Nights

Whenever the moon and stars are set,
  Whenever the wind is high,
All night long in the dark and wet,
  A man goes riding by.
Late in the night when the fires are out,
Why does he gallop and gallop about?

Whenever the trees are crying aloud,
  And ships are tossed at sea,
By, on the highway, low and loud,
  By at the gallop goes he.
By at the gallop he goes, and then
By he comes back at the gallop again.

ROBERT LOUIS STEVENSON

Lullaby

The long canoe
Toward the shadowy shore,
One . . . two . . .
Three . . . four . . .
The paddle dips,
Turns in the wake,
Pauses, then
Forward again,
Water drips
From the blade to the lake.
Nothing but that,
No sound of wings;
The owl and bat
Are velvet things.
No wind awakes,
No fishes leap,
No rabbits creep
Among the brakes.

The long canoe
At the shadowy shore,
One . . . two . . .
Three . . . four . . .
A murmur now
Under the prow
Where rushes bow
To let us through.
One . . . two . . .
Upon the shore,
Three . . . four . . .
Upon the lake,
No one's awake,
No one's awake,
One . . .
Two . . .
No one,
Not even
You.

ROBERT HILLYER

·39·

ACKNOWLEDGMENTS

The editor and publisher have made every effort to trace the ownership of all copyrighted material and to secure permission from holders of such copyrights. In the event of any question arising as to the use of any material, the publisher and editor, while expressing regret for inadvertent error, will be pleased to make the necessary corrections in future printings. Thanks are due to the following authors, publishers, and agents for permission to use the material indicated.

"Baby Toes" from *Smoke and Steel* by Carl Sandburg, copyright 1920 by Harcourt, Inc. and renewed 1948 by Carl Sandburg. Reprinted by permission of the publisher.

"The Bridge" from *I Thought I Heard the City* by Lilian Moore. Copyright © 1969, 1997 by Lilian Moore. Used by permission of Marian Reiner for the author.

"The Frog" from *Cats and Bats and Things With Wings*. Copyright © 1965 by Conrad Aiken, copyright © 1993 by Joan Aiken and Jane Aiken Hodge. Reprinted by permission of Brandt & Brandt Literary Agents, Inc.

"The Gentle Giant" from *Jelly Belly* (Macmillan of Canada, 1983). Copyright © 1983 by Dennis Lee. With permission of the author.

"Lullaby" from *Poems for Music 1917–1947* by Robert Hillyer, copyright 1947 by Robert Hillyer and renewed 1975 by Francesca P. Hillyer and Elizabeth V. Hillyer. Recorded by permission of Alfred A. Knopf Inc. Used by permission of Alfred A. Knopf, a division of Random House, Inc.

"Manhattan Lullaby" by Norma Farber, copyright © by Tom Farber. Used by permission.

"The Moon's the North Wind's Cooky" reprinted with the permission of Scribner, a Division of Simon & Schuster, from *Collected Poems* by Vachel Lindsay (New York: Macmillan, 1925).

"The Mouse," from *Compass Rose* by Elizabeth Coatsworth, copyright 1929 by Coward-McCann, Inc., renewed © 1957 by Elizabeth Coatsworth. Used by permission of Coward-McCann, an imprint of Penguin Putnam Books for Young Readers, a division of Penguin Putnam Inc.

"Nightfall" copyright © 1992 by Barbara Juster Esbensen. Used by permission of HarperCollins Publishers.

"Questions at Night" from *Rainbow in the Sky* by Louis Untermeyer, copyright 1935 by Harcourt, Inc. and renewed 1963 by Louis Untermeyer. Reprinted by permission of the publisher.

"The Starlighter" from *Gaily the Troubadour* by Arthur Guiterman (New York: E.P. Dutton, 1936). Reprinted with the permission of Louise H. Sclove.

"The yellow fog . . ." from "The Love Song of J. Alfred Prufrock" from *Collected Poems 1901–1962* by T. S. Eliot, copyright 1936 by Harcourt, Inc., copyright © 1964, 1963 by T. S. Eliot. Reprinted by permission of the publisher.